AI, Robotics and Mechatronics

The Future of Work:
Human-Robot Collaboration

Ava Kai Renn

Table of Contents

Introduction

The landscape of work is undergoing a transformation unlike anything humanity has seen before. Machines that once served as simple tools are now evolving into intelligent collaborators, capable of thinking, analyzing, and performing tasks with remarkable precision. Artificial intelligence, robotics, and mechatronics are not just reshaping industries—they are redefining the relationship between humans and technology in profound and unprecedented ways.

At the heart of this change lies the concept of human-robot collaboration. This isn't about machines replacing people. It's about forging a partnership where humans and robots complement each other's strengths, creating a synergy that drives innovation and efficiency. Robots excel at repetitive, high-precision tasks, while humans bring creativity, empathy, and critical thinking to the table. Together, they are setting the stage for a future where the impossible becomes possible.

However, this future comes with challenges. Ethical dilemmas, safety concerns, and the fear of obsolescence weigh heavily on the minds of workers and leaders alike. Questions about trust, adaptability, and the redistribution of labor demand immediate attention. Yet, these challenges are not insurmountable; they represent opportunities to rethink, reinvent, and reimagine the world of work.

This book presents a vision of how humans and robots can work side by side, harmonizing technology with humanity to build a better future. From the advancements driving these changes to the strategies for overcoming obstacles, every page is dedicated to understanding and navigating this pivotal moment in history.

The future of work is not distant or abstract—it is happening now. The decisions we make today will define how this partnership evolves and what it means for generations to come. Together, humans and robots have the power to achieve greatness, creating workplaces that are more efficient, equitable, and enriching. This is not just the next chapter of work; it is a new era.

Part 1: Foundations of AI, Robotics, and Mechatronics

Chapter 1

Understanding AI and Machine Learning

Artificial Intelligence (AI) and Machine Learning (ML) have transitioned from theoretical concepts to transformative forces shaping every facet of modern life. AI refers to the ability of machines to mimic human intelligence, solving problems, making decisions, and even understanding natural language. Machine Learning, a subset of AI, empowers systems to improve their performance over time by learning from data rather than being explicitly programmed. Together, these technologies are at the forefront of innovation, driving advancements in industries ranging from healthcare to finance, manufacturing to entertainment. Understanding these concepts is essential not only to appreciate their potential but also to recognize the profound impact they have on the present and future of work.

The integration of AI and ML into daily operations and complex systems is changing the way organizations function. Businesses are leveraging predictive analytics, recommendation systems, and automated processes to enhance productivity and decision-making. As AI systems become more advanced, they are taking on tasks that were once considered uniquely human, such as interpreting emotions or diagnosing diseases. This section begins with a foundational understanding of AI's core principles and then dives into how Machine Learning enables machines to learn and evolve autonomously. It concludes by addressing one of the most pressing concerns in AI—its ethical implications and the balance between innovation and responsibility.

The Core Concepts of Artificial Intelligence

Artificial Intelligence is more than just machines executing commands. It encompasses the ability to perceive, reason, and act with purpose. At its core, AI seeks to replicate human cognitive functions through algorithms and computational models. From autonomous vehicles navigating complex road systems to AI-powered chatbots resolving customer queries, the scope of AI applications continues to expand. Yet, the key to AI's capabilities lies in its ability to process and analyze vast amounts of data, extracting patterns and making predictions with incredible speed and accuracy.

Central to AI's functionality are technologies like natural language processing (NLP), which allows machines to understand and generate human language, and computer vision, enabling systems to interpret visual data from the world around them. Another critical component is neural networks, modeled after the human brain's structure, which form the foundation for deep learning. These advancements empower machines to perform tasks like speech recognition, facial recognition, and real-time language translation.

AI operates across two primary categories: narrow AI and general AI. Narrow AI, the most prevalent form today, is designed to perform specific tasks, such as voice recognition in virtual assistants like Siri or Alexa. General AI, on the other hand, represents a more ambitious goal—creating machines capable of performing any intellectual task a human can do. Although general AI remains theoretical, ongoing research is pushing its boundaries.

The effectiveness of AI hinges on data. Algorithms process enormous datasets to identify trends, correlations, and insights. For example, in healthcare, AI analyzes patient records and medical images to detect anomalies, predict diseases, and recommend treatments. In finance, it predicts market trends and detects fraudulent transactions. The ability to harness data is what makes AI so powerful, but it also raises questions about privacy and data security, which are explored in later discussions.

Beyond applications, AI's strength lies in its adaptability. Unlike traditional software, AI systems can refine their processes through feedback, learning from past errors, and improving their performance. This capability is vital in dynamic environments where conditions constantly change, such as supply chain management or autonomous vehicles navigating traffic. AI's adaptability ensures that it remains relevant and effective across industries and use cases.

However, AI is not without limitations. Machines lack emotional intelligence and the ability to understand context in the way humans do. While they excel at tasks requiring data processing, they fall short in areas requiring empathy, moral reasoning, and complex problem-solving. This underscores the importance of human oversight and collaboration, ensuring that AI serves as a tool to augment human capabilities rather than replace them.

Understanding the core concepts of AI allows us to appreciate its immense potential while remaining aware of its boundaries. It is this duality—its power and its limitations—that makes AI one of the most intriguing and impactful technologies of our time. As we progress through this chapter, the focus shifts to Machine Learning, the driving force behind AI's ability to learn and improve, and its role in shaping intelligent systems.

Machine Learning: Training Machines to Learn

Machine Learning represents the backbone of modern Artificial Intelligence, transforming static programming into dynamic systems capable of adapting to new information. At its essence, Machine Learning enables machines to learn from data and improve their performance over time without being explicitly programmed for every scenario. This ability has revolutionized industries by creating systems that are not only efficient but also predictive and responsive.

The process begins with feeding algorithms vast datasets, which they analyze to detect patterns and relationships. Supervised learning, one of the most common forms of Machine Learning, involves training models on labeled data, where inputs and their corresponding outputs are clearly defined. This method is widely used in applications such as spam detection, image recognition, and predictive text generation. On the other hand, unsupervised learning identifies hidden patterns in data without predefined labels, making it ideal for clustering and segmentation tasks, like customer segmentation in marketing.

A more advanced form, reinforcement learning, focuses on decision-making processes. Here, algorithms learn by interacting with an environment and receiving feedback in the form of rewards or penalties. This approach has been instrumental in developing AI systems capable of playing complex games like chess or Go and optimizing robotic movements in manufacturing. Each method showcases the versatility and adaptability of Machine Learning across different domains.

While Machine Learning algorithms are powerful, their success is heavily reliant on the quality and quantity of data they process. Poor-quality data can lead to biased or inaccurate models, resulting in flawed outcomes. Ensuring data integrity and addressing biases are critical challenges that developers must navigate to harness the full potential of Machine Learning.

The applications of Machine Learning extend far beyond theoretical scenarios. In healthcare, predictive models analyze patient histories to forecast potential illnesses, enabling early interventions. In e-commerce, recommendation systems suggest products based on a user's browsing and purchasing history, enhancing the shopping experience. Financial institutions leverage Machine Learning to detect fraudulent activities in real time, safeguarding transactions and building customer trust.

Machine Learning's ability to handle complex datasets and provide actionable insights has made it an indispensable tool in decision-making. For instance, in supply chain management, algorithms predict demand fluctuations, optimize inventory, and streamline logistics, ensuring efficiency and cost savings. In urban planning, Machine Learning analyzes traffic patterns to propose solutions for congestion and pollution reduction.

However, Machine Learning also introduces challenges. The "black box" nature of some algorithms, where decision-making processes are not easily interpretable, raises concerns about transparency and accountability. Additionally, the energy consumption associated with training large models has sparked debates about the environmental impact of AI technologies. Addressing these issues requires a balanced approach, prioritizing innovation while upholding ethical standards.

The future of Machine Learning holds immense promise, with advancements in neural networks, quantum computing, and edge AI poised to expand its capabilities even further. By equipping machines with the ability to learn, adapt, and improve, Machine Learning is not only redefining technology but also reshaping the way we work, interact, and solve problems.

The discussion on Machine Learning lays the groundwork for understanding the ethical considerations that arise when implementing AI systems. As technology becomes more integrated into daily life, addressing its moral and societal implications is imperative to ensure a future where innovation benefits all.

Chapter 2

Robotics: The Mechanized Workforce

Robotics has transcended its roots in science fiction to become an integral part of modern industry and society. From automating repetitive tasks to performing complex operations, robots have redefined what machines can achieve. These intelligent mechanical systems are no longer confined to assembly lines; they are now found in hospitals, homes, agriculture, and even outer space. Robotics represents a blend of engineering, programming, and innovation, driving advancements that enable machines to operate autonomously or collaboratively alongside humans.

The rise of robotics has been fueled by breakthroughs in technology, including advancements in sensors, artificial intelligence, and materials science. These developments have made robots more precise, reliable, and adaptable, expanding their potential applications. However, robotics is not just about replacing human effort; it's about augmenting human capabilities, enhancing efficiency, and opening doors to possibilities that were once unimaginable. This chapter explores the journey of robotics, the components that define modern machines, and their transformative impact across industries.

The Evolution of Robotics

The journey of robotics begins with the concept of automating tasks, an idea that dates back centuries. Early automated devices, like the water clocks of ancient civilizations and mechanical automatons of the Renaissance, laid the foundation for modern robotics.

However, it wasn't until the industrial revolution that the idea of mechanized labor began to take shape, paving the way for the first wave of robotic innovation.

The advent of digital technology in the 20th century marked a turning point. In 1954, George Devol invented the first programmable robot, the Unimate, which was later employed in General Motors' production lines to perform tasks such as welding and material handling. This ushered in the era of industrial robots, designed to improve productivity and reduce costs in manufacturing. These early robots were limited in capability but set the stage for rapid advancements in the decades to come.

The introduction of microprocessors and advancements in computing in the 1970s and 1980s enabled robots to become more intelligent and versatile. They could now perform tasks requiring greater precision and flexibility, such as assembling electronic components. Collaborative robots, or cobots, emerged in the late 1990s, designed to work alongside humans rather than replace them. This marked a shift from purely industrial applications to broader possibilities, including healthcare, education, and service industries.

Today, robotics is entering its most dynamic phase. Advances in artificial intelligence, machine learning, and machine vision have enabled robots to perform complex tasks, such as surgery, autonomous navigation, and even social interaction. Soft robotics, which uses flexible materials to mimic biological movements, has expanded the scope of robotics into delicate tasks like handling fragile objects or assisting in rehabilitation therapies. The evolution of robotics reflects humanity's ability to push the boundaries of technology and apply it to solve real-world challenges.

Key Components of Modern Robots

Modern robots are sophisticated systems comprising multiple components that work in harmony to perform tasks. At the heart of every robot lies its mechanical structure, which provides the physical framework for movement and interaction. This structure, often designed with materials like aluminum, carbon fiber, or plastic, determines the robot's durability, flexibility, and application.

Actuators and motors are critical components that enable robots to move and manipulate objects. These devices convert electrical signals into mechanical motion, allowing robots to perform actions such as lifting, rotating, or gripping. Advances in motor technology, including servo motors and hydraulic actuators, have significantly improved the precision and power of modern robots.

Sensors serve as the robot's "eyes and ears," enabling it to perceive its environment and respond accordingly. Cameras, LiDAR systems, and proximity sensors allow robots to detect obstacles, measure distances, and navigate complex spaces. Tactile sensors and force feedback mechanisms enhance a robot's ability to interact with objects, ensuring safe and effective operations in dynamic environments.

The control system acts as the brain of the robot, processing data from sensors and issuing commands to actuators. This system relies on algorithms and software that determine the robot's behavior based on inputs and desired outcomes. In recent years, the integration of artificial intelligence has enhanced robots' decision-making capabilities, enabling them to learn from experience and adapt to new tasks.

Power supply is another vital component, determining the robot's operating time and mobility. While stationary robots often rely on wired power sources, mobile robots use batteries or fuel cells for energy. Innovations in energy storage, such as lithium-ion batteries, have extended the operational range and efficiency of modern robots.

Finally, communication systems enable robots to interact with other devices, systems, or humans. Wireless connectivity, such as Wi-Fi and Bluetooth, allows robots to exchange data in real-time, coordinate actions, and operate as part of a larger network. This connectivity is essential for collaborative robots and autonomous systems that rely on constant communication to function effectively.

Applications Across Industries

The applications of robotics span virtually every industry, transforming processes and redefining possibilities. In manufacturing, robots have become indispensable for tasks such as assembly, welding, and quality inspection. Their precision, speed, and ability to work in hazardous environments have revolutionized production lines, enabling higher efficiency and lower costs.

In healthcare, robotics is making a profound impact, particularly in surgical procedures. Robotic-assisted surgeries allow for minimally invasive operations, reducing recovery times and improving patient outcomes. Robots are also used in rehabilitation, assisting patients in regaining mobility, and in elder care, providing companionship and support.

Agriculture has embraced robotics to address labor shortages and increase productivity. Autonomous tractors, drones, and robotic harvesters are optimizing planting, irrigation, and harvesting processes. These technologies are not only improving yields but also enabling sustainable farming practices by reducing resource waste.

In logistics and warehousing, robots are enhancing efficiency by automating tasks like sorting, packing, and transportation. Autonomous mobile robots (AMRs) navigate warehouses, retrieve items, and streamline inventory management. Companies like Amazon and DHL have adopted these systems to meet the demands of e-commerce and fast delivery expectations.

Service industries are increasingly utilizing robots for customer interaction and support. From hotel concierge robots that assist guests to robotic baristas that prepare coffee, these applications demonstrate how robots are becoming a part of everyday life. In education, robots are being used to teach coding, provide interactive lessons, and support students with special needs.

Even in hazardous environments, robots are proving invaluable. They are deployed in disaster response, performing search-and-rescue operations in areas unsafe for humans. In space exploration, robots like the Mars rovers conduct scientific research on other planets, expanding our understanding of the universe.

The potential applications of robotics are virtually limitless. As technology continues to advance, robots will play an even greater role in shaping industries and improving lives. Their integration into the workforce underscores the importance of understanding their capabilities and limitations, ensuring they are used responsibly and effectively.

Chapter 3

Mechatronics: The Intersection of Mechanics and Electronics

Mechatronics represents a revolutionary field that seamlessly combines mechanical engineering, electronics, computer science, and control systems to create sophisticated and intelligent systems. It is not merely a blend of these disciplines but a transformative approach to designing machines and systems that can sense, think, and act. From automated manufacturing processes to autonomous vehicles, mechatronics has become the backbone of modern engineering solutions.

At its core, mechatronics aims to enhance the functionality, precision, and efficiency of systems by integrating mechanical and electronic components with smart control strategies. This synergy has opened new frontiers in automation, robotics, and advanced machinery, making processes more efficient and less labor-intensive. This chapter introduces the concept of mechatronics, highlights innovations in integrated systems, and explores its impact on real-world applications that are shaping industries and daily life.

What Is Mechatronics?

Mechatronics is the multidisciplinary field that focuses on the integration of mechanical systems with electronic components and intelligent control mechanisms. While traditional mechanical systems relied on manual or rudimentary automated controls, mechatronics introduces electronics and software into the equation, enabling machines to perform complex tasks autonomously or with minimal human intervention.

The term "mechatronics" originated in Japan during the 1960s, reflecting the need to create systems that combined mechanics and electronics. Over time, the field expanded to include computer science and control systems, enabling the development of systems capable of adaptive and intelligent behavior. Mechatronics has since evolved into a cornerstone of modern engineering, underpinning technologies as diverse as precision manufacturing tools, smart home devices, and autonomous vehicles.

A key aspect of mechatronics is its emphasis on system integration. This means designing systems where mechanical components, sensors, actuators, and controllers work seamlessly together to achieve a desired outcome. For example, in an autonomous drone, the mechanical structure enables flight, sensors provide environmental data, actuators control movement, and the onboard computer processes information to navigate safely.

In addition to creating new systems, mechatronics has also revolutionized existing technologies. By integrating electronics and intelligence into mechanical designs, engineers have significantly improved the performance, reliability, and versatility of machines. The field continues to evolve, driven by advances in areas such as microelectronics, artificial intelligence, and the Internet of Things (IoT).

Innovations in Integrated Systems

The integration of mechanics and electronics has led to groundbreaking innovations, redefining what machines can achieve. At the heart of mechatronics lies the concept of sensors and actuators working in unison with advanced control systems. These components enable machines to sense their environment, process information, and perform precise actions in real time, resulting in systems that are both efficient and adaptive.

One significant innovation in mechatronics is the development of advanced control algorithms. These algorithms allow machines to optimize their performance dynamically, adjusting to changes in the environment or operational conditions. For instance, in industrial robotics, control algorithms ensure that robotic arms can adapt to variations in assembly tasks without requiring manual reprogramming.

Another breakthrough is the miniaturization of components. The integration of microelectromechanical systems (MEMS) has enabled the development of compact sensors and actuators, which are essential for applications like wearable devices and medical implants. These tiny systems combine mechanical and electronic elements on a microscopic scale, opening up possibilities in fields such as healthcare, where minimally invasive technologies are critical.

The Internet of Things (IoT) has further transformed mechatronics by enabling systems to communicate and interact through networks. IoT-connected devices can share data, receive updates, and coordinate their actions remotely, creating smarter and more interconnected systems. This has profound implications for industries like logistics, where IoT-enabled machines can optimize supply chain operations in real-time.

Artificial intelligence (AI) and machine learning have also become integral to mechatronic systems. By incorporating AI, machines can analyze data, recognize patterns, and make decisions autonomously. For example, in autonomous vehicles, AI processes sensor data to navigate complex environments, avoiding obstacles and adhering to traffic rules.

This level of intelligence is a testament to how far integrated systems have come.

Energy efficiency is another area where mechatronics has made significant strides. Modern mechatronic systems incorporate energy-saving technologies such as regenerative braking in electric vehicles, where energy lost during braking is captured and reused. This focus on sustainability ensures that machines are not only high-performing but also environmentally friendly.

The integration of augmented reality (AR) and virtual reality (VR) with mechatronics is unlocking new possibilities in training, design, and remote operations. Engineers can now use AR to visualize and interact with complex systems in real-time, making it easier to troubleshoot and optimize performance. These technologies are also transforming how machines are developed, with simulations allowing for more efficient design and testing processes.

Real-World Mechatronics Applications

The impact of mechatronics is evident in a wide range of applications, demonstrating its versatility and transformative potential. In the automotive industry, mechatronics plays a pivotal role in the development of advanced driver-assistance systems (ADAS), electric vehicles, and autonomous cars. Features like adaptive cruise control, lane-keeping assistance, and automated parking rely on the seamless integration of sensors, actuators, and control systems.

In the manufacturing sector, mechatronics has revolutionized production processes through the introduction of smart factories. These facilities use robots, automated conveyors, and

IoT-enabled machines to optimize operations, reduce waste, and increase productivity. Mechatronic systems also enable predictive maintenance, where machines can monitor their own health and alert operators to potential issues before they escalate.

The healthcare industry benefits greatly from mechatronics, particularly in the design of medical devices and robotic systems. Surgical robots, for example, allow for minimally invasive procedures with unparalleled precision. Prosthetics and exoskeletons equipped with sensors and actuators provide mobility and independence to individuals with physical disabilities, enhancing their quality of life.

In the aerospace and defense sectors, mechatronics is critical for the development of unmanned aerial vehicles (UAVs), missile guidance systems, and spacecraft. These applications require systems that can operate reliably under extreme conditions, showcasing the robustness and adaptability of mechatronic designs.

Mechatronics is also transforming the agriculture industry through the development of precision farming technologies. Automated tractors, robotic harvesters, and smart irrigation systems optimize resource usage and increase crop yields, addressing the challenges of food security and environmental sustainability.

In everyday life, mechatronics is present in smart home devices, such as automated lighting, thermostats, and security systems. These systems use sensors and control algorithms to create comfortable, safe, and energy-efficient living environments. Wearable devices like fitness trackers and smartwatches are another example, combining mechanics, electronics, and software to monitor health metrics and enhance personal well-being.

The field of mechatronics continues to push boundaries, finding new applications in areas as diverse as renewable energy, education, and entertainment. By enabling systems that are intelligent, efficient, and adaptable, mechatronics is shaping a future where technology enhances every aspect of human life.

Part 2: The Role of Collaboration in the Future of Work

Chapter 4

The Human Touch: Why Collaboration Matters

The rapid advancements in robotics and artificial intelligence have revolutionized industries and redefined the possibilities of automation. Machines have taken on tasks that were once exclusively performed by humans, offering precision, speed, and tireless operation. Despite these breakthroughs, the essence of human ingenuity, adaptability, and emotional intelligence cannot be replicated by machines. This chapter emphasizes the indispensable value of human-robot collaboration and how it enhances productivity, innovation, and workplace harmony. By understanding the unique strengths and limitations of both humans and machines, we can craft a future where collaboration leads to unprecedented achievements.

The partnership between humans and robots is not merely a technical integration but a nuanced relationship that balances efficiency with creativity, logic with empathy, and predictability with adaptability. This interplay highlights why the human touch remains critical even in a robot-driven world. By leveraging the best of both realms, industries are discovering how collaboration fosters a dynamic environment where each counterpart complements the other's strengths.

The Limitations of Automation

Automation has revolutionized many industries, streamlining processes, reducing errors, and enhancing efficiency. However, even the most sophisticated robots have inherent limitations that restrict their capabilities. These machines excel in executing repetitive tasks, analyzing large datasets, and maintaining precision, but their lack of flexibility and creativity hinders them from navigating ambiguous or novel situations effectively.

One key limitation of automation lies in its dependency on preprogrammed instructions. Robots and AI systems function based on algorithms designed to handle specific scenarios, making them ill-suited for tasks requiring improvisation or abstract thinking. For instance, while a robot can assemble components with flawless accuracy, it cannot redesign a process when faced with an unexpected challenge or inefficiency.

Another significant drawback of automation is its inability to connect emotionally or socially. Robots lack empathy, intuition, and the ability to interpret subtle human cues, which are essential in professions like healthcare, customer service, and education. A robot might efficiently administer medication or provide information, but it cannot comfort a distressed patient or inspire a struggling student.

The absence of ethical reasoning and moral judgment further limits automation's role in decision-making. AI systems operate based on data and logic, but they lack the context or ethical framework needed to evaluate complex societal or cultural implications. This limitation underscores the importance of human oversight, particularly in applications like law enforcement, financial decision-making, and public policy.

Moreover, automation struggles with tasks requiring a high degree of sensory perception or fine motor skills in unstructured environments. Robots may excel in controlled settings like factories but often falter in unpredictable or dynamic environments such as construction sites or natural disaster zones. These shortcomings highlight why human involvement remains critical in scenarios where adaptability and nuanced understanding are essential.

Strengths of Human Workers in a Robot-Driven World

While robots bring unparalleled efficiency and precision to the table, human workers possess qualities that machines cannot replicate. Creativity, emotional intelligence, and problem-solving skills remain uniquely human attributes that are vital for innovation and meaningful collaboration. In a robot-driven world, the strengths of human workers lie in their ability to adapt, connect, and envision.

Humans excel in creativity and critical thinking, qualities that drive innovation and problem-solving. Unlike robots, which rely on existing data and algorithms, humans can think abstractly, question assumptions, and generate original ideas. These strengths are particularly valuable in fields like research, design, and strategy, where creative solutions and long-term vision are essential.

Empathy and interpersonal skills set humans apart in roles that require emotional connection and relationship-building. In sectors like healthcare, counseling, and hospitality, the ability to understand and respond to the emotional needs of others fosters trust and enhances the quality of service. Robots may provide assistance, but human warmth and intuition create experiences that resonate deeply with individuals.

The human ability to adapt to unforeseen circumstances is another irreplaceable strength. In dynamic or high-pressure situations, humans can evaluate context, make quick decisions, and pivot strategies as needed. This adaptability is particularly critical in emergency response, conflict resolution, and crisis management, where rigid algorithms fall short.

Collaboration and teamwork also highlight human strengths. Humans can communicate, negotiate, and build consensus, enabling them to work effectively in diverse teams. These skills are crucial when integrating robots into the workplace, as humans must guide, train, and oversee their robotic counterparts to ensure seamless operation.

Ethical reasoning and moral judgment further demonstrate the importance of human involvement. Decisions that impact lives or societal norms require a nuanced understanding of values, culture, and context—factors that robots cannot comprehend. This ensures that humans remain the ultimate decision-makers in sensitive or complex scenarios.

Case Studies in Effective Human-Robot Collaboration

Real-world examples of human-robot collaboration illustrate the transformative potential of this partnership. Across industries, businesses and organizations have successfully integrated robots to complement human workers, enhancing productivity, safety, and innovation. These case studies provide valuable insights into how collaboration can shape the future of work.

In the manufacturing sector, companies like BMW and Tesla have implemented "cobots"—collaborative robots designed to work alongside human employees. These robots handle repetitive and physically demanding tasks, such as assembly and welding, while human workers focus on quality control, troubleshooting, and creative problem-solving. This synergy not only increases efficiency but also improves workplace safety by reducing human exposure to hazardous conditions.

The healthcare industry has seen remarkable advancements through human-robot collaboration. In hospitals, robotic surgical systems like the da Vinci Surgical System assist surgeons by providing enhanced precision and stability during procedures. While the robot performs intricate movements, the surgeon retains full control and oversight, ensuring optimal patient outcomes. Similarly, robots in elder care facilities support caregivers by assisting with tasks like lifting patients or delivering supplies, allowing staff to dedicate more time to emotional and social interactions.

In agriculture, the integration of robots and human expertise is transforming farming practices. Autonomous tractors, drones, and robotic harvesters optimize planting, irrigation, and crop monitoring. Farmers use data collected by these machines to make informed decisions about resource allocation and crop management, combining technology with their knowledge of local conditions and agricultural practices.

The logistics and warehousing sector has also benefited from human-robot collaboration. Companies like Amazon and FedEx use robotic systems to sort and transport packages within their facilities. Human workers oversee operations, manage exceptions, and ensure that customer service standards are met. This partnership enhances efficiency while maintaining the flexibility needed to handle unique challenges.

In construction, robots assist workers by performing tasks like bricklaying, concrete pouring, and demolition. These machines reduce physical strain on human laborers and allow them to focus on tasks requiring creativity, judgment, and precision. The collaboration between humans and robots in construction projects accelerates timelines and improves overall quality.

By combining the strengths of humans and robots, these case studies demonstrate how collaboration can lead to transformative results. Rather than viewing automation as a replacement for human labor, industries are increasingly recognizing it as a powerful tool that enhances human capabilities and enriches the workplace.

Chapter 5

AI and Robotics in the Workplace

Artificial intelligence and robotics are no longer the technologies of the future—they are the transformative forces of today. Across industries, these innovations are reshaping how work is performed, boosting efficiency, enhancing precision, and redefining human roles. The integration of AI and robotics into workplaces has created opportunities for growth and innovation while presenting challenges that demand adaptation and strategic foresight. This chapter examines the profound impact of AI and robotics in the workplace, the rise of collaborative robots, and the necessity of preparing the workforce for this evolving landscape.

As businesses embrace AI and robotics, they are finding new ways to optimize operations and deliver value. These technologies are not simply replacing tasks but are also creating new roles and opportunities for collaboration. The synergy between human creativity and robotic efficiency is unlocking possibilities that were once deemed unattainable. Yet, the rapid pace of technological change raises important questions about the future of work, skill development, and the balance between innovation and humanity.

Transforming Industries: Manufacturing, Healthcare, and Beyond

The transformative impact of AI and robotics is most evident in industries like manufacturing, where automation has revolutionized production processes. Robots equipped with AI capabilities perform repetitive, precise, and hazardous tasks, enabling factories to operate around the clock. In automotive manufacturing, for instance, robots handle assembly, welding, and painting with a level of speed and accuracy that exceeds human capacity. These advancements not only reduce costs but also enhance product quality and workplace safety.

In healthcare, robotics and AI are making life-saving contributions. Surgical robots assist doctors with minimally invasive procedures, providing greater precision and reducing recovery times for patients. AI-powered systems analyze medical data to detect patterns, enabling earlier diagnosis of diseases such as cancer. Robots in elder care help caregivers with physical tasks, allowing them to focus on emotional and relational aspects of care. These innovations are improving patient outcomes and addressing labor shortages in critical areas.

Retail and logistics have also embraced AI and robotics to meet rising consumer demands. Robots in warehouses sort, pack, and transport goods, significantly speeding up delivery times. AI-driven inventory systems predict customer needs and optimize stock levels, reducing waste and ensuring timely availability. In the retail space, robots assist with tasks like shelf stocking and customer inquiries, enhancing the shopping experience while freeing up human employees for more complex roles.

Agriculture, another traditionally labor-intensive industry, has benefited immensely from robotics and AI. Autonomous tractors and drones are transforming farming practices, optimizing planting and harvesting processes, and conserving resources like water and fertilizer. AI systems analyze weather patterns, soil conditions, and crop health, enabling farmers to make informed decisions and improve yields. These advancements contribute to sustainable practices and address the global demand for food security.

Education and training have also seen the influence of AI and robotics. Virtual teaching assistants powered by AI support educators by handling administrative tasks and providing personalized learning experiences for students. Robots in classrooms enhance engagement, particularly for STEM education, by offering hands-on opportunities for learning coding and engineering. These tools are preparing the next generation to thrive in an increasingly technology-driven world.

The entertainment industry is another domain where AI and robotics are making strides. Robots are used in film production, stage performances, and interactive installations, creating experiences that were previously unimaginable. AI algorithms power content recommendations, gaming experiences, and even the creation of music and art, broadening the scope of creativity and personalization.

Collaborative Robots (Cobots) on the Rise

Collaborative robots, or cobots, represent a significant shift in how machines are integrated into workplaces. Unlike traditional industrial robots, which operate in isolated environments, cobots are designed to work alongside humans. This new generation of robots emphasizes partnership, combining human creativity and decision-making with robotic precision and efficiency. Cobots are making inroads across various sectors, transforming the way work is done.

Cobots are particularly impactful in manufacturing, where they handle repetitive or physically demanding tasks while allowing human workers to focus on quality control and problem-solving. For example, in assembly lines, cobots can perform tasks like screwing, welding, or packaging, reducing the strain on human workers and increasing overall productivity. By working collaboratively, humans and cobots achieve results that neither could accomplish alone.

In healthcare, cobots assist with patient care by performing tasks such as lifting, transferring, and dispensing medication. These robots reduce the physical burden on healthcare workers and improve safety for patients. Cobots are also used in physical therapy, where they guide patients through rehabilitation exercises with precision and consistency. Their presence enables caregivers to devote more attention to emotional support and patient well-being.

Retail environments have seen the introduction of cobots for inventory management and customer service. Cobots equipped with sensors and AI algorithms can navigate store aisles, monitor stock levels, and guide customers to products. Their ability to operate in dynamic, people-filled spaces demonstrates the advancements in robotic sensing and interaction technologies.

The agricultural sector benefits from cobots as well. These robots perform tasks like harvesting delicate crops, planting seeds, and sorting produce. Cobots work alongside farmers to improve efficiency while minimizing crop damage, ensuring higher yields and reduced waste. Their integration addresses the challenges of labor shortages and the growing demand for sustainable farming practices.

The rise of cobots underscores the importance of designing systems that prioritize safety, ease of use, and adaptability. With advanced sensors and AI algorithms, cobots are capable of detecting human presence, adjusting their actions, and learning from their environment.

This makes them valuable assets in industries seeking to balance automation with human-centric approaches.

Preparing the Workforce for Integration

The integration of AI and robotics into workplaces demands a workforce that is ready to adapt and thrive in a technology-driven environment. Preparing employees for this transition involves fostering a mindset of lifelong learning, equipping them with relevant skills, and addressing the social and ethical implications of automation. This preparation is essential to ensure that the benefits of technology are realized without compromising human dignity and purpose.

Reskilling and upskilling initiatives are critical for helping workers navigate the changing landscape. Training programs in fields such as robotics, data analysis, and AI programming empower employees to take on new roles and responsibilities. Additionally, emphasizing soft skills like critical thinking, creativity, and emotional intelligence ensures that human workers retain their competitive edge in areas where machines fall short.

Education systems must evolve to equip future generations with the tools needed for a technology-driven world. Schools and universities should emphasize STEM subjects, as well as interdisciplinary fields like mechatronics and human-robot interaction. Early exposure to coding, robotics, and AI concepts prepares students to engage with emerging technologies and fosters a culture of innovation.

Workplace environments must also embrace a culture of collaboration and inclusivity. Encouraging cross-functional teams where humans and robots work together fosters mutual understanding and trust. Providing employees with hands-on experience and training in working alongside robots reduces apprehension and builds confidence in their ability to adapt.

Addressing the ethical and societal implications of automation is equally important. Organizations must ensure that the integration of AI and robotics aligns with values like fairness, transparency, and inclusivity. Policies and regulations should be developed to protect workers' rights and ensure equitable access to the benefits of automation.

Preparing the workforce for integration also involves fostering a sense of purpose and resilience. As automation takes on repetitive tasks, workers should be encouraged to focus on roles that involve creativity, strategy, and interpersonal connection. This shift highlights the importance of human-centric work and the value of collaboration in achieving meaningful outcomes.

Chapter 6

Rethinking Skills and Education

The rapid evolution of AI, robotics, and mechatronics is reshaping the fabric of work and society, demanding a fundamental reevaluation of how we prepare for the future. Traditional education models, designed for a static industrial era, are increasingly inadequate in a world defined by continuous innovation and disruption. The skills needed to thrive today—and tomorrow—transcend rote knowledge, requiring a blend of technical expertise, creativity, and emotional intelligence. This chapter addresses the future of skills and education, emphasizing the necessity of bridging skill gaps and embracing lifelong learning in a fast-changing world.

The intersection of technology and education presents both challenges and opportunities. As industries transform, the gap between the skills employers need and the skills workers possess continues to widen. At the same time, the potential for education to adapt and innovate has never been greater. Whether through reimagined curriculums, immersive technologies, or flexible learning pathways, the future of skills and education lies in aligning human capabilities with technological advancements.

The Future Skillset: Technical, Creative, and Emotional Intelligence

The demands of the modern workplace extend far beyond technical proficiency. While expertise in fields such as AI programming, data analytics, and robotics engineering remains essential, it is creativity and emotional intelligence that set humans apart from machines. These uniquely human qualities enable innovation, adaptability, and collaboration—skills that are indispensable in an automated world.

Technical skills serve as the foundation for navigating a tech-driven environment. Understanding programming languages, AI algorithms, and system integration allows individuals to work alongside intelligent machines effectively. For instance, data scientists translate complex information into actionable insights, while robotics engineers design systems that enhance productivity and safety. As technology continues to advance, proficiency in emerging fields such as quantum computing and bioinformatics will become increasingly valuable.

Creativity is equally critical, enabling individuals to approach problems from fresh perspectives and develop solutions that transcend conventional boundaries. Designers, innovators, and strategists use their imagination to bridge gaps between technology and user needs. In industries such as healthcare, creative thinkers are driving advancements in personalized medicine, while in entertainment, they are redefining how stories are told through AI-generated art and interactive media.

Emotional intelligence amplifies the effectiveness of technical and creative skills by fostering empathy, communication, and collaboration. In roles requiring customer interaction, for example, emotional intelligence ensures that human connections remain central to service delivery. Leaders who demonstrate emotional intelligence are better equipped to navigate change, inspire teams, and create inclusive environments where both humans and machines can thrive.

Balancing these three pillars—technical, creative, and emotional—creates a skillset that is resilient and future-ready. As automation handles repetitive tasks, humans will be free to focus on areas that require judgment, ingenuity, and interpersonal understanding, ensuring their indispensability in the workplace.

Bridging the Skills Gap: Training for Tomorrow

The skills gap represents a critical challenge as industries adopt AI and robotics at unprecedented speeds. Many workers find themselves ill-equipped to meet the demands of a rapidly changing job market, while businesses struggle to fill positions requiring specialized expertise. Addressing this gap requires coordinated efforts from governments, educational institutions, and employers.

Training programs tailored to emerging technologies are essential for equipping workers with relevant skills. Partnerships between industries and academic institutions can create targeted curriculums that align with market needs. For example, apprenticeship programs in robotics provide hands-on experience, allowing participants to learn while contributing to real-world projects. Short-term boot camps and certification courses offer focused training in areas like machine learning, empowering workers to upskill quickly.

Government initiatives play a pivotal role in addressing systemic challenges. Policies that fund reskilling programs, subsidize education, and incentivize businesses to invest in employee development create pathways for workforce adaptation. By prioritizing inclusion, these initiatives ensure that opportunities are accessible to all, particularly marginalized groups who may face barriers to entry.

Employers must also commit to fostering a culture of continuous learning. Offering on-the-job training, mentorship programs, and professional development opportunities empowers employees to grow alongside technological advancements. Companies that invest in their workforce not only retain talent but also position themselves as leaders in innovation and adaptability.

Bridging the skills gap requires a forward-thinking approach that anticipates future needs rather than reacting to current trends. Predictive analytics and labor market forecasting tools can identify emerging skills, allowing educators and employers to align efforts proactively. This anticipatory mindset ensures that individuals are prepared for opportunities before they arise, reducing the risk of obsolescence.

Lifelong Learning in a Fast-Changing World

In a world defined by constant change, the concept of education as a one-time endeavor is obsolete. Lifelong learning has become a necessity, enabling individuals to adapt, grow, and remain relevant throughout their careers. This paradigm shift emphasizes curiosity, adaptability, and a commitment to personal and professional development.

Lifelong learning begins with fostering a growth mindset—the belief that abilities can be developed through dedication and effort. Individuals who embrace this mindset are more likely to pursue opportunities for learning, even in the face of challenges. Whether acquiring new technical skills, mastering creative tools, or enhancing interpersonal abilities, lifelong learners approach education as an ongoing journey.

Digital platforms have revolutionized access to education, making lifelong learning more feasible than ever before. Online courses, webinars, and virtual workshops provide flexible options for skill development, allowing individuals to learn at their own pace. Platforms like Coursera, edX, and LinkedIn Learning offer courses on cutting-edge topics, connecting learners with expertise from global institutions.

Workplace environments that encourage continuous learning foster resilience and innovation. Providing employees with access to training resources, workshops, and peer-to-peer learning opportunities creates a culture of growth. Organizations that prioritize learning not only enhance their competitiveness but also empower their workforce to thrive in the face of change.

Lifelong learning also requires adaptability to new educational formats and tools. Immersive technologies like virtual reality (VR) and augmented reality (AR) enable experiential learning, making complex concepts accessible and engaging. AI-driven learning platforms personalize educational experiences, tailoring content to individual needs and preferences. These advancements enhance both the effectiveness and enjoyment of lifelong education.

Ultimately, lifelong learning is about more than acquiring skills; it is about cultivating a mindset of curiosity and resilience. In a fast-changing world, those who remain open to learning are better equipped to seize opportunities, overcome challenges, and shape the future. This commitment to growth ensures that individuals, industries, and societies can navigate the complexities of a technology-driven era with confidence and purpose.

Part 3:
Challenges and
Opportunities
in
Human-Robot
Collaboration

Chapter 7

Ethics and Trust in Human-Robot Interactions

As human-robot interactions become increasingly common in workplaces, homes, and public spaces, the dynamics of trust and ethics take center stage. Robots are no longer confined to factory floors; they now serve as companions, caregivers, and coworkers. While these interactions hold immense potential for improving efficiency and quality of life, they also raise critical questions about trust, safety, and ethical responsibility. This chapter examines how trust can be established between humans and machines, the imperative of ensuring safety in collaborative environments, and the ethical complexities posed by intelligent systems.

In an era defined by rapid technological advancements, trust becomes the foundation for successful human-robot partnerships. Without trust, even the most advanced systems will face resistance and underutilization. Similarly, ethical principles must guide the development and deployment of these technologies, ensuring they align with human values and priorities. Together, trust and ethics form the cornerstone of a harmonious and responsible future where humans and machines work side by side.

Building Trust Between Humans and Machines

Trust is a crucial element in any relationship, including those involving humans and robots. For individuals to feel comfortable working alongside machines, they must believe in the reliability, transparency, and intentions of these systems. Building trust in human-robot interactions is a multifaceted process that involves technical, psychological, and social considerations.

Reliability is one of the primary factors influencing trust. Robots must perform their tasks consistently and predictably to gain the confidence of their human counterparts. Whether it is a surgical robot assisting in delicate procedures or a warehouse robot managing inventory, predictable performance reassures users of the machine's competence. Regular maintenance, robust software updates, and rigorous testing ensure that robots function without failure, further reinforcing reliability.

Transparency is equally vital in fostering trust. Humans need to understand how robots make decisions, especially in high-stakes environments. Explainable AI, a field focused on making machine learning algorithms interpretable, plays a critical role here. For example, a self-driving car that can explain why it made a particular maneuver can ease concerns about its decision-making process. Open communication about a robot's limitations and capabilities also helps set realistic expectations.

Social behaviors also contribute to trust-building. Robots designed with human-like gestures, voice tones, or facial expressions can create a sense of familiarity and comfort. In settings such as healthcare or elder care, these attributes make interactions feel more personal, fostering emotional connections between humans and machines. However, these designs must avoid creating unrealistic perceptions of a robot's intelligence or autonomy, as misplaced trust can lead to overreliance and unintended risks.

The process of building trust is ongoing, requiring consistent positive experiences. Users need time to acclimate to new technologies and gain confidence through interaction. By addressing reliability, transparency, and social dynamics, designers and engineers can ensure that trust becomes a natural outcome of human-robot partnerships.

Ensuring Safety in Collaborative Environments

Safety is the cornerstone of ethical human-robot interactions, especially in environments where humans and machines work side by side. Collaborative robots, or cobots, are designed to operate alongside humans, performing tasks that augment human capabilities rather than replacing them. Ensuring safety in these settings requires a combination of advanced technology, thoughtful design, and robust regulatory frameworks.

Modern robots are equipped with sophisticated sensors and algorithms that enable them to detect and respond to their surroundings. Proximity sensors, cameras, and lidar technology allow robots to perceive human presence and adjust their actions accordingly. For example, a cobot in a manufacturing plant can slow down or halt its movements if a worker comes too close, minimizing the risk of accidents.

Ergonomic design is another critical aspect of safety. Robots should be designed with soft edges, padded surfaces, or flexible components to reduce the impact of accidental contact. Additionally, intuitive interfaces and controls empower human operators to manage robots effectively, preventing errors that could compromise safety.

Regulatory standards play a crucial role in maintaining safety. Organizations such as the International Organization for Standardization

(ISO) and the Occupational Safety and Health Administration (OSHA) establish guidelines for the design, deployment, and operation of robots. Compliance with these standards ensures that safety remains a top priority across industries.

Continuous monitoring and evaluation are essential for maintaining safety in collaborative environments. Machine learning algorithms can analyze data from sensors to identify patterns that signal potential risks. By detecting and addressing these risks in real time, robots can adapt to changing conditions and maintain a safe working environment.

Ultimately, ensuring safety is not solely a technical challenge—it is also a matter of fostering a culture of awareness and accountability. Workers must receive adequate training to understand the capabilities and limitations of the robots they interact with. Similarly, developers and manufacturers must prioritize safety at every stage of a robot's lifecycle, from design to decommissioning.

The Ethical Challenges of Intelligent Systems

The rise of intelligent systems brings with it a host of ethical challenges that demand careful consideration. These challenges arise from the unprecedented capabilities of AI and robotics, which blur the lines between human and machine agency. Addressing these ethical dilemmas is critical to ensuring that technological progress aligns with societal values and promotes the greater good.

One of the most pressing ethical concerns is bias in AI systems. Machine learning algorithms are only as unbiased as the data they are trained on. If the training data reflects existing societal inequalities, the resulting systems can perpetuate or even amplify these biases. For instance, facial recognition technologies have been criticized for their higher error rates in identifying individuals with darker skin tones. Addressing bias requires diverse datasets, transparent algorithms, and ongoing audits to ensure fairness and inclusivity.

Privacy is another major ethical issue. Robots and intelligent systems often rely on data collection to function effectively. Whether it is a home assistant recording voice commands or a healthcare robot accessing medical records, the potential for misuse of sensitive information is significant. Robust data protection policies, encryption, and user consent protocols are essential for safeguarding privacy in human-robot interactions.

Autonomy and accountability present unique ethical challenges. As robots become more capable of making decisions independently, determining responsibility for their actions becomes increasingly complex. For example, in the case of a self-driving car involved in an accident, should the blame fall on the manufacturer, the software developer, or the car itself? Establishing clear frameworks for accountability ensures that ethical considerations keep pace with technological advancements.

The potential displacement of human workers by robots also raises ethical questions about economic inequality and social responsibility. While automation can enhance productivity, it can also lead to job losses, particularly in low-skilled roles. Policymakers, businesses, and educators must collaborate to ensure that technological progress benefits society as a whole, rather than exacerbating disparities.

Navigating the ethical challenges of intelligent systems requires a multidisciplinary approach that brings together technologists, ethicists, policymakers, and the public. By fostering open dialogue and prioritizing ethical considerations, society can harness the benefits of AI and robotics while minimizing their risks and unintended consequences.

Chapter 8

Overcoming Barriers to Adoption

The widespread adoption of robotics, AI, and mechatronics is transforming industries and reshaping societies. However, this transformative journey is not without challenges. Economic constraints, cultural resistance, and technological complexities present significant barriers to widespread adoption. Additionally, fear and skepticism about these advancements often hinder progress, slowing the pace of integration. Understanding and addressing these barriers is essential for unlocking the full potential of these technologies and ensuring that their benefits are equitably distributed. This chapter examines the hurdles to adoption, the resistance to change, and the strategies for fostering smooth integration in various sectors.

Economic, Cultural, and Technological Hurdles

Adopting robotics and AI often involves substantial economic investments, which can be prohibitive for smaller businesses or developing economies. The costs of acquiring advanced systems, maintaining them, and training employees to operate them create a financial burden. For instance, manufacturing firms may hesitate to invest in robotic systems due to high upfront costs, even if these technologies promise long-term savings. Governments and private entities must collaborate to provide financial incentives, subsidies, and accessible financing options to encourage adoption.

Cultural hurdles further complicate the adoption process. Societal attitudes toward automation and robotics vary significantly across regions and industries. In some cultures, a deep-rooted skepticism about replacing human labor with machines fuels resistance. Traditional industries, such as agriculture in rural areas, often view robotics as intrusive rather than beneficial. Overcoming cultural barriers requires targeted education and awareness campaigns that highlight the advantages of robotics while addressing fears about job displacement and societal impacts.

Technological barriers also play a significant role in slowing adoption. Many organizations lack the infrastructure required to support advanced technologies. For example, integrating robotics in logistics requires seamless connectivity, advanced software, and robust cybersecurity measures. Additionally, gaps in technical expertise among the workforce can hinder implementation.

Bridging these gaps demands substantial investments in research, infrastructure, and skills development, ensuring that technological advancements are accessible and effective for diverse applications.

Addressing Fear and Resistance to Change

Fear and resistance to change are perhaps the most significant barriers to adopting robotics and AI. The fear of job displacement looms large, with many workers concerned that robots will render their roles obsolete. This anxiety is particularly acute in industries where automation has already replaced manual tasks, such as manufacturing and logistics. To address these fears, organizations must emphasize the role of technology as an enabler rather than a replacement for human labor.

Transparency and communication are key to easing resistance. Leaders must openly discuss the motivations for adopting robotics and AI, outlining the specific benefits for both the organization and its workforce. Employees should be reassured that these technologies are intended to enhance productivity, improve safety, and create new opportunities, rather than eliminate jobs. For instance, robotic systems can handle repetitive or hazardous tasks, allowing human workers to focus on more complex and creative activities.

Offering reskilling and upskilling opportunities is another effective strategy for reducing resistance. Employees are more likely to embrace change when they feel equipped to navigate the new landscape. Training programs should focus on developing the technical skills required to work alongside robots and AI, as well as soft skills like adaptability and problem-solving. By investing in their workforce, organizations can foster a culture of trust and collaboration.

Collaborative robots, or cobots, serve as a practical solution for addressing resistance. Unlike traditional industrial robots, cobots are designed to work alongside humans, enhancing their capabilities rather than replacing them. These machines demonstrate the potential for harmonious human-robot collaboration, easing fears and building acceptance.

Strategies for Smooth Integration

Successfully integrating robotics and AI into existing systems requires a strategic approach that balances innovation with operational continuity. The first step is conducting a thorough needs assessment to identify specific areas where technology can provide the most value. This analysis ensures that investments are targeted and aligned with organizational goals, minimizing disruptions during the transition.

Pilot programs are a practical way to test and refine new technologies before full-scale deployment. For instance, a retail chain might introduce AI-driven inventory management in a few stores to evaluate its effectiveness. Feedback from these pilot programs can inform adjustments, ensuring that the technology is optimized for broader implementation.

Cross-disciplinary collaboration is essential for smooth integration. Engineers, managers, IT specialists, and end-users must work together to address technical and operational challenges. This collaborative approach ensures that diverse perspectives are considered, reducing the likelihood of oversights and ensuring that solutions are practical and user-friendly.

Investing in infrastructure is a critical component of integration. Robust networks, cloud computing capabilities, and advanced cybersecurity measures are essential for supporting the complex requirements of robotics and AI. Additionally, organizations must establish clear protocols for maintenance, updates, and troubleshooting to ensure long-term success.

Change management strategies play a crucial role in facilitating adoption. Organizations must prioritize communication, providing clear information about the timeline, objectives, and expected outcomes of the integration process. Workshops, town hall meetings, and training sessions can help build support among employees, ensuring that they feel engaged and valued throughout the transition.

Ultimately, the successful integration of robotics and AI requires a forward-thinking mindset that balances technological advancement with human-centric considerations. By addressing economic, cultural, and technological hurdles, alleviating fears and resistance, and implementing strategic integration plans, organizations can harness the full potential of these transformative technologies. This approach not only ensures operational success but also paves the way for a more inclusive and innovative future.

Chapter 9

Opportunities for Innovation and Growth

The world is at the cusp of a new era where human-robot collaboration is not just a possibility, but a reality shaping industries across the globe. With advancements in artificial intelligence, robotics, and mechatronics, organizations are finding new ways to work smarter, more efficiently, and more creatively. These technologies offer a wealth of opportunities for innovation and growth, giving businesses the tools to stay competitive in a rapidly changing world. The potential for transformative change is immense, from enhancing productivity to fostering groundbreaking creativity. In this chapter, we will examine how these advancements are driving human-robot partnerships, redefining the concept of productivity, and offering new pathways to building a sustainable future for all.

Advancements Driving Human-Robot Partnerships

As robotics and AI technologies continue to evolve, their integration into the workforce opens doors for novel forms of collaboration between humans and machines. One of the most significant advancements is the development of collaborative robots, or cobots, which are specifically designed to work alongside human operators. Unlike traditional robots, which are often isolated from humans, cobots are created to assist and complement human abilities. This partnership allows robots to take over repetitive or hazardous tasks, freeing human workers to focus on tasks requiring creativity, emotional intelligence, and complex decision-making.

Furthermore, AI has become an essential component in driving the effectiveness of these collaborations. By enabling robots to "learn" from their environment and improve their performance over time, AI helps bridge the gap between human intelligence and machine precision. Through machine learning and deep learning algorithms, robots are becoming better at adapting to new tasks, refining their processes, and even making real-time decisions based on their surroundings. This collaboration between human ingenuity and machine efficiency results in more productive and dynamic work environments.

Robots are also becoming more capable of understanding and responding to human input, through advanced sensors, vision systems, and speech recognition. These features allow for more intuitive interaction between humans and robots, enhancing the ease with which they can work together. As these systems become smarter and more flexible, the potential for truly seamless human-robot partnerships grows, pushing the boundaries of what is possible in fields ranging from manufacturing to healthcare to service industries.

Redefining Productivity and Creativity

The growing presence of robots and AI is not just improving efficiency in the workplace; it is also redefining productivity itself. In traditional models of productivity, success has often been measured by output per unit of labor—how many products are made or how quickly tasks are completed. While this is still important, the rise of robotics has shifted the focus towards value-added work, where the combination of human creativity and machine precision creates higher-quality outcomes and more innovative products.

AI and robotics can handle repetitive, data-intensive, and time-consuming tasks that would otherwise take human workers countless hours. This automation allows individuals to shift their focus towards more meaningful and intellectually stimulating work, fostering a creative environment where ideas can flow and innovations can emerge. In creative industries, such as design, art, and entertainment, AI and robotics are being harnessed to push boundaries and explore new possibilities. Designers are using AI-powered tools to generate unique patterns and designs, while robotics is enhancing capabilities in creating complex physical art forms.

Moreover, this shift in the definition of productivity opens up new opportunities for human workers to embrace roles that were once thought to be outside the realm of their abilities. Creative problem-solving, emotional intelligence, and empathy—skills that are uniquely human—are becoming increasingly important in the workplace, allowing individuals to add value in ways that machines cannot. Rather than being displaced by automation, workers are empowered to contribute in areas where they excel, while robots take care of the more routine and mundane tasks.

This shift in focus towards creativity and innovation is not limited to the arts and design. In fields like research and development, AI and robotics are enabling more rapid prototyping, hypothesis testing, and even personalized innovation. Scientists and engineers can now experiment with ideas and solutions more quickly, using AI to analyze data and robots to build physical prototypes, cutting down the time needed to bring new concepts to life. This rapid iteration process accelerates progress, fostering an environment where innovation is the norm, not the exception.

Building a Sustainable Future Together

As industries become increasingly reliant on robotics and AI, one of the key challenges that must be addressed is sustainability. The integration of advanced technologies offers significant opportunities for making operations more environmentally friendly and socially responsible. Robotics, for instance, can play a vital role in creating sustainable solutions by optimizing resource use and minimizing waste. By employing precision and efficiency, robots can help reduce energy consumption, streamline production processes, and contribute to more sustainable manufacturing practices.

In agriculture, robots are being developed to assist with everything from planting to harvesting, reducing the need for harmful pesticides and fertilizers, and increasing crop yields while minimizing environmental impact. Similarly, in the energy sector, robots are being deployed for tasks such as inspecting solar panels, maintaining wind turbines, and monitoring the health of electrical grids, helping to optimize the use of renewable energy sources.

AI is also making strides in the fight against climate change. By analyzing vast amounts of environmental data, AI algorithms can predict trends, optimize energy distribution, and identify potential risks to ecosystems. In conjunction with robotics, AI is being used to clean up pollution, restore ecosystems, and manage natural resources more efficiently, paving the way for a more sustainable future.

However, the move towards a sustainable future is not just about reducing environmental harm; it is also about creating socially responsible technologies that benefit everyone. In the realm of human-robot collaboration, sustainability involves ensuring that the technologies are accessible to a wide range of people and industries, from large corporations to small enterprises, and that they are used in ways that promote economic and social equity. This means focusing on training and reskilling programs that equip workers with the skills needed to thrive in this new environment and ensure that no one is left behind in the transition.

As businesses and governments invest in these technologies, they must also commit to making ethical choices that prioritize the well-being of society as a whole. By incorporating sustainable practices into the development and deployment of robotics and AI, we can help create a future where innovation and growth go hand in hand with environmental stewardship and social responsibility. The collaboration between humans and machines holds the key to this future, with robots and AI acting as partners that support and enhance human efforts to build a better, more sustainable world for generations to come.

Part 4: Looking Ahead

Chapter 10

The Next Frontier: AI, Robotics, and Society

As we move forward into an era where artificial intelligence, robotics, and mechatronics are integral parts of our daily lives, it is crucial to consider the broader implications these technologies will have on both our work and personal lives. These innovations promise transformative changes to how we work, communicate, and interact with one another. As we venture into this new frontier, we must also examine the challenges and opportunities that will arise. Predicting the future of work and life, understanding the role of policy and regulation, and fostering global collaboration will be key to navigating this rapidly evolving landscape. In this chapter, we will explore these pivotal aspects, providing insights into how AI and robotics will reshape society and what we can do to ensure that these changes are beneficial for all.

Predicting the Future of Work and Life

The integration of AI and robotics into our work environments is already reshaping industries and altering traditional job structures. In the future, we will likely witness an acceleration of these changes, with many routine tasks automated by machines, allowing humans to engage in more creative and strategic work. Automation will not only change the nature of jobs but also redefine entire industries, creating new fields of work while making others obsolete. However, this transition will not be without its challenges. While automation can lead to higher productivity and efficiency, it will also require substantial adaptation from workers and organizations alike.

One significant aspect of this transformation will be the need for workers to continuously update their skill sets to stay relevant in an AI-driven world. As more industries embrace automation, workers will be expected to adapt to new technologies and develop complementary skills that are uniquely human, such as creativity, critical thinking, and emotional intelligence. This means that the future workforce will likely see an increased emphasis on lifelong learning, with individuals taking responsibility for their own personal and professional development throughout their careers.

The workplace itself will also undergo significant changes. With AI and robotics handling many tasks, human workers will increasingly collaborate with machines, leading to a more fluid and dynamic work environment. Remote work and flexible schedules, already popularized by technology in recent years, will continue to evolve, facilitated by AI-driven platforms that enhance communication, collaboration, and productivity. As robots and AI become more advanced, they will seamlessly integrate into our daily routines, creating an environment where humans and machines work together in harmony.

Beyond the workplace, the influence of AI and robotics will extend to nearly every aspect of our lives. From smart homes that anticipate our needs to AI-driven healthcare systems that provide personalized treatment, these technologies will enhance our quality of life and revolutionize how we interact with the world. As AI systems become more intuitive, they will integrate into our personal lives, making decisions on our behalf, managing resources, and even offering companionship. While this raises important ethical questions about privacy and autonomy, it also holds great promise for improving accessibility and convenience in daily life.

The Role of Policy and Regulation in Shaping Innovation

As the rapid pace of AI and robotics development continues, governments, industries, and societies must implement thoughtful policies and regulations to guide innovation. Without clear regulatory frameworks, the deployment of these technologies could result in unintended consequences, such as widening inequalities or stifling innovation in certain sectors. Effective policies must balance the need to foster technological advancements with the responsibility to address social, ethical, and economic challenges.

One of the primary concerns regarding AI and robotics is the potential for job displacement. While automation can lead to greater efficiency, it can also result in workers being replaced by machines, particularly in industries that rely on repetitive tasks. Policymakers must address these challenges by implementing measures that protect workers while promoting the adoption of AI technologies. This includes supporting retraining programs to help workers transition to new roles, investing in education to prepare future generations for the workforce of tomorrow, and introducing safety nets to mitigate the impacts of displacement.

Another key area for regulation is the ethical use of AI and robotics. As machines become more autonomous, they will increasingly make decisions that affect people's lives, such as in healthcare, law enforcement, and transportation. It is critical that policies are put in place to ensure that these systems operate fairly, transparently, and with accountability.

For instance, ethical guidelines should govern the use of AI in sensitive areas like criminal justice to prevent bias, discrimination, and abuse of power. Governments must work closely with technologists, ethicists, and other stakeholders to ensure that these systems adhere to the highest standards of ethics and human rights.

Data privacy is also a major concern in the age of AI and robotics. With machines gathering and processing vast amounts of personal data, it is essential for policymakers to establish robust frameworks for data protection. Regulations should ensure that individuals have control over their personal information and are informed about how their data is being used. Striking the right balance between privacy and the need for data to power AI systems is one of the greatest challenges in shaping the future of these technologies.

Fostering Global Collaboration for Progress

The future of AI and robotics holds tremendous potential for improving lives across the globe. However, to fully realize the benefits of these technologies, international cooperation will be essential. Collaboration among governments, private sectors, and academic institutions will foster innovation and create shared standards for AI and robotics development. Global partnerships will also be necessary to address the common challenges posed by these technologies, such as job displacement, ethical concerns, and data privacy.

One of the key benefits of global collaboration is the opportunity to pool resources, knowledge, and expertise. By working together, countries can accelerate the development of AI and robotics while ensuring that these technologies are accessible and beneficial to all.

This collaborative approach can also help bridge the digital divide between developed and developing nations, ensuring that everyone has access to the advantages these technologies offer. International research initiatives, such as those focused on AI in healthcare or environmental sustainability, can create shared solutions to global problems, benefiting all of humanity.

International cooperation also plays a vital role in setting global standards for the ethical and responsible use of AI and robotics. As these technologies become more widespread, it will be crucial for countries to agree on common frameworks that ensure they are used in ways that promote fairness, transparency, and accountability. Global standards will help prevent the fragmentation of regulatory systems and encourage uniformity in how these technologies are deployed across borders.

Furthermore, fostering global collaboration can help create a collective vision for the future of work and life in an AI-driven world. By engaging in dialogue across cultures, industries, and political systems, we can ensure that the evolution of AI and robotics benefits everyone, rather than exacerbating existing inequalities. The future of AI, robotics, and society is not something that can be achieved in isolation; it will require a concerted effort from all corners of the globe to create a fair and inclusive future.

In conclusion, the next frontier of AI, robotics, and society is filled with both tremendous opportunities and significant challenges. As we look ahead, it is clear that the technologies we are developing today will shape the world of tomorrow. To ensure that these advancements benefit all of humanity, we must carefully navigate the complexities of predicting the future of work, crafting thoughtful policies, and fostering global collaboration. By doing so, we can harness the power of AI and robotics to create a better, more equitable future for all.

Chapter 11

A Vision for a Collaborative Future

As artificial intelligence, robotics, and mechatronics continue to transform industries and reshape how we live and work, it's important to embrace the vision of a future built on human-robot collaboration. In this future, machines will not replace human workers but enhance their abilities, allowing people to focus on higher-level tasks that require creativity, emotional intelligence, and problem-solving skills. The convergence of human potential with machine efficiency will create a new era of productivity, innovation, and fulfillment. This vision requires a shift in mindset, moving from the fear of obsolescence to the recognition that technology can be a powerful ally in achieving collective success.

Rather than viewing robots as competitors, we must see them as partners that complement our unique strengths. A collaborative future is one where humans and machines work side by side to tackle the challenges of today while creating new opportunities for growth and development.

The future of work will be characterized by dynamic and evolving roles that blend the technical with the creative. Workers will increasingly rely on robots and AI systems to handle repetitive, dangerous, or mundane tasks, freeing up human resources to engage in more fulfilling, strategic, and human-centric activities. Industries will shift from traditional hierarchical structures to more fluid and collaborative environments, where both human workers and machines play integral roles in achieving common goals. This vision of a shared workforce holds great promise for a more inclusive, innovative, and sustainable future. As we embrace this collaboration, we can redefine what success means in the workplace and society at large, measuring it not just by output but by the positive impact we make together, as humans and machines, in our shared journey toward progress.

Redefining Success in a Shared Workforce

In the past, success in the workforce has often been defined by individual accomplishments, measured in terms of promotions, salary increases, and productivity. However, as AI and robotics shift the landscape, the definition of success will evolve to reflect a more collaborative and holistic approach. In a world where humans work alongside machines, success will no longer be determined solely by personal output, but by the ability to contribute to a collective goal. It will be measured by how well humans and robots can work together, leveraging each other's strengths to drive innovation, efficiency, and well-being.

Redefining success also means recognizing that the traditional barriers between manual and intellectual labor will blur. Jobs that once required human dexterity or physical strength will be augmented by robotics, while tasks that required complex reasoning will be enhanced by AI. As such, success in the future workforce will depend not on the ability to outperform others but on the capacity to integrate technological advancements into everyday work processes. The workforce of tomorrow will value adaptability, creativity, and emotional intelligence—skills that machines are less likely to master in the near future. By redefining success in this way, we can build a workplace that celebrates collaboration, creativity, and continuous learning, where both humans and machines thrive.

Empowering Humans Through Technology

As we look toward the future, it is essential to understand that technology, particularly AI and robotics, has the potential to empower humans, not replace them. The key lies in leveraging these innovations to augment human abilities rather than undermine them. Technology can provide individuals with tools that expand their reach, improve decision-making, and enhance their productivity. In a collaborative environment, robots can take on repetitive, tedious tasks, allowing humans to focus on areas where they excel—problem-solving, emotional intelligence, and leadership.

Empowerment through technology also means that workers can have more control over their work-life balance. Automation can alleviate the burden of monotonous or physically demanding jobs, opening up new possibilities for personal and professional fulfillment. Technology will not only make jobs safer and more efficient but will also enable workers to access better training, upskilling opportunities, and career pathways. By embracing technological advancements, workers can become more agile, adaptable, and prepared for the challenges of a rapidly changing world. Empowerment, in this sense, means that technology is a tool for liberation—freeing individuals from tasks that drain their energy and creativity, allowing them to flourish in their roles and contribute to the success of their organizations and society.

Imagining the Workplace of Tomorrow

The workplace of tomorrow will look vastly different from today, shaped by advances in AI, robotics, and mechatronics. Rather than a sterile, isolated environment, the workplace will be a dynamic space that fosters collaboration between humans and machines. Physical offices may give way to hybrid or fully remote setups, where workers engage with robots and AI systems through intuitive interfaces and collaborative platforms. In this new environment, technology will serve as a seamless extension of human capabilities, enhancing productivity, communication, and creativity.

Workplaces will no longer be defined by rigid structures and hierarchical organizations. Instead, teams will be more fluid, with humans and machines working together to solve complex problems. Robots may handle routine tasks, such as inventory management or data analysis, while human workers focus on higher-level decision-making, strategic planning, and interpersonal interactions. The office itself will be designed to foster collaboration, creativity, and well-being, with spaces dedicated to both focused work and team collaboration. Technology will enable workers to access information and tools from anywhere, at any time, making the workplace more flexible and adaptable to individual needs and preferences.

One of the most significant changes in the workplace of tomorrow will be the integration of AI-driven decision-making. Rather than relying solely on human judgment, teams will make data-informed decisions in real-time, supported by insights generated by advanced algorithms. This will enable more agile decision-making processes, faster problem-solving, and more personalized experiences for employees and customers alike. However, as this shift occurs, it will be essential to maintain a focus on human creativity and empathy, qualities that machines cannot replicate. The workplace of the future will be one where technology and human ingenuity intersect, leading to a more efficient, innovative, and fulfilling environment for all involved.

Conclusion

As we stand on the cusp of a new era—where artificial intelligence, robotics, and mechatronics converge to redefine the very fabric of our society—it is essential to celebrate the profound potential these innovations hold. The transformative power of AI and robotics is not just about technological advancements; it's about how these tools can enhance our humanity, unlock new realms of creativity, and forge deeper connections in the workplace and beyond. The future we envision is one of collaboration, where humans and machines work in harmony, complementing each other's strengths to create a world that is not only more efficient but more compassionate, inclusive, and innovative.

Together, we have the opportunity to embrace this future with open arms, guided by a commitment to ethical standards, continuous learning, and an unwavering belief in our collective potential. The challenges ahead are significant, but the rewards are immeasurable. By fostering a culture of collaboration, adaptability, and empowerment, we can navigate the complexities of an AI-driven world and create a society where every individual has the opportunity to thrive.

In the end, the true success of this technological revolution will be measured not by the machines we create but by the progress we make as a human race. We have the power to shape a future where technology serves as a tool for liberation, enabling us to focus on what matters most—our shared humanity, our capacity for creativity, and our unwavering desire to make the world a better place for future generations. The journey ahead is an exciting one, full of boundless possibilities. Together, let's take the first step toward a brighter, more connected tomorrow.